Quetzals

By Sandra Donovan

Steadwell Books

Raintree Steck-Vaughn Publishers

A Harcourt Company

Austin · New York

www.raintreesteckvaughn.com

ANIMALS OF THE RAIN FOREST

Library of Congress Cataloging-in-Publication Data
ISBN: 0-7398-5530-1
Printed and bound in the United States of America
1 2 3 4 5 6 7 8 9 10 WZ 05 04 03 02

Published by Raintree Steck-Vaughn Publishers,
an imprint of Steck-Vaughn Company.

Produced by Compass Books

Photo Acknowledgments
All photos by Michael and Patricia Fogden.

Editor: Bryon Cahill
Consultant: Sean Dolan

Content Consultant
Brian Schwartz, Cloudforest Alive

This book supports the National Science Standards.

Contents

MEXICO

BELIZE
HONDURAS
NICARAGUA
Caribbean
Sea

North
Atlantic
Ocean

GUATEMALA
EL SALVADOR

COSTA RICA

PANAMA

ECUADOR

VENEZUELA

COLOMBIA

GUYANA
SURINAME
FRENCH
GUIANA
(FRANCE)

PERU

AMAZON
RIVER

BRAZIL

BOLIVIA

South
Pacific
Ocean

CHILE

PARAGUAY

South
Atlantic
Ocean

ARGENTINA

URUGUAY

Range of
the Quetzal

Surrounding
Land

Water

Borders

Rivers

N
W   E
S

What do quetzals look like?

Quetzals are colorful birds. They are bright green with yellow beaks. Males have bright red stomachs and long green tail feathers. Females have gray stomachs and short tails.

Where do quetzals live?

Quetzals live in the forests of Central America and South America.

What do quetzals eat?

Quetzals eat more than 40 different kinds of fruit. They also may eat insects, frogs, snails, small lizards, and other meat.

The quetzal eats fruits and plants that grow in the rain forest.

Quetzals in the Rain Forest

Many people have called quetzals the most beautiful birds in the world. Birds are warm-blooded animals that have a backbone, wings, feathers, and a beak. Warm-blooded animals have a body temperature that stays the same, no matter what the temperature is outside.

The full name for quetzals is resplendent (ree-SPLEND-ent) quetzals. Resplendent means brightly shining. Scientists call quetzals *Pharomachrus mocinno* (FAYR-oh-MAHK-ris muh-CHEEN-oh).

Quetzals live in rain forests. A rain forest is a warm place where many different trees and plants grow close together, and a lot of rain falls. Quetzals are important to the rain forest because they help some plants to grow. They do this by spreading the seeds of the plants that they eat to new places. The seeds leave their bodies in their waste.

This male quetzal is resting on a branch in the rain forest.

Where Do Quetzals Live?

Quetzals live in the rain forests of Central America and South America, mostly in the countries of Costa Rica and Guatemala. They may also be found in parts of Mexico, Honduras, El Salvador, and Panama.

Many quetzals make their homes very high up in the mountains. This area is called the cloud forest because it is so high that clouds cover the rain forests for days at a time.

Quetzals do not live in the cloud forest all year. They move to a new **habitat** when the seasons change. A habitat is the area where an animal lives or a plant naturally grows. Moving to a new habitat like this is called **migrating**.

There are only two seasons in the rain forest. These are the dry season and the rainy season. These seasons begin at different times, depending on where the forest is. In some places, the dry season lasts from December to April. During these months, quetzals live in the cloud forest. It is usually wet in the cloud forest. Even when it does not rain, there is a lot of cloud mist that keeps the plants and trees wet.

After April, the rainy season begins. During these months, a great deal of rain falls. Quetzals often leave the cloud forest in July. They move to the lowland areas of the rain forest where it is warmer and drier. In December or January, they fly back to the cloud forest to live. Some quetzals will stay in the cloud forest all year long if there is enough food.

Nests and Territories

Quetzals usually make their nests anywhere from 14 to 90 feet (4 to 27 m) above the ground. Sometimes they live in tree-hole nests made by other birds, such as toucans or parrots. Other times, they will build their nests themselves inside of dead trees. They use dead trees because the rotted wood is soft—their beaks are not strong enough to make a hole in a hard, living tree. With their beak, quetzals hollow out a small opening to crawl through. Then, they carve out a larger area behind the opening. They line the bottom of the opening with leaves.

Most quetzals live in the same area of the rain forest, but they do not live together. This is because quetzals are territorial animals. Territorial means that an animal lives in one area, or territory, and protects it from other animals. Male quetzals each have their own territory. They may fight to protect their area from other male quetzals as well as from other kinds of animals.

There is only one time during the year when a male and female quetzal will live together. This

> ▲ **This quetzal is about to enter its nest. The nest is inside the hole in the tree.**

is during the mating season. The mating season is usually just before the rainy season begins. The quetzal pair stays together to raise the chicks. Then, they leave each other to live alone again.

You can see the crest and bright yellow beak of this male quetzal.

What Do Quetzals Look Like?

Quetzals are very colorful birds. They have a shiny green head, back, and wings. Some of the feathers on their tail are white. The upper feathers are bright green or blue. They also have a bright yellow beak.

Male quetzals and female quetzals have slightly different coloring. Male quetzals have a bright red stomach. They also have a crest of feathers on their head. A crest is a row of feathers that stands up straight like a mohawk haircut. Female quetzals are not as colorful as males. Their stomach is more gray than red.

Male quetzals are known for four long green feathers on their tail. They are called **coverts**. Coverts can grow more than 2 feet (60 cm) long. Females have a short tail without coverts.

Both male and female quetzals grow to be about 14 inches (36 cm) long. They weigh about 8 ounces (210 g). When male quetzals fly, they can be up to 3 feet (90 cm) long. This is because of their long tail feathers. Because coverts are so long, some people say that male quetzals look like flying snakes.

A quetzal's wings are specially built for flying in the forest. Their wings are curved. This shape helps them to make sharp turns. They can also quickly fly higher or lower. With their special wings, they can swoop in and out of the treetops.

Quetzals have special feet, too. Their first and second toe faces backward. This helps them grip tree branches.

This female quetzal is eating a wild avocado.

What Quetzals Eat

Quetzals are **omnivores**. An omnivore is an animal that eats both plants and animals. Younger quetzals will mainly eat animals, while adult quetzals will eat plants. Young quetzals eat small lizards, frogs, snails, and insects. They need the protein from meat to grow up strong. After they grow up, quetzals eat mostly fruits.

Adult quetzals eat more than 40 different kinds of fruit. Their most common food is the avocado. Avocados are green fruits with a large seed in the center. Quetzals eat whole avocados, and then they regurgitate the seed. To regurgitate means to bring food back up from the stomach and out of the mouth. They regurgitate the seed because their body cannot break it down.

Quetzals have no teeth, so they swallow their food whole.

Finding and Eating Food

Quetzals eat fruit from the trees where they live. They usually do not have trouble finding food. It grows all around them in the rain forest. When food becomes hard to find, they migrate from one area to another during the year.

In the rainy season, quetzals live high up in the cloud forest where many kinds of avocado are plentiful. During this season, there are almost 12 different kinds of avocado that grow in the cloud forest. Quetzals eat almost all of these kinds.

By the beginning of the dry season, it becomes harder to find avocados in the cloud forest. This is when quetzals migrate to lower areas of the rain forest. In these areas, other kinds of avocado are then ripe and ready to eat.

Once quetzals find food, they use their beak to tear small pieces from it. They swallow their food whole. Like all birds, quetzals do not have teeth. A special body part called a gizzard grinds up their food. Quetzals swallow small stones and other objects. These objects stay in the gizzard, which is near the stomach. Large pieces of food roll around with the hard objects in the gizzard. This grinds the food into small pieces.

Often quetzals regurgitate large avocado seeds far away from the plants where they grew. This spreads avocado plants throughout the rain forest. In this way, quetzals help to keep the rain forests alive.

This male quetzal is digging out a tree-hole nest with its beak.

A Quetzal's Life Cycle

Most quetzals mate once a year in the spring. Some quetzals mate twice a year, once in the spring and once in the summer.

Male quetzals court female quetzals. To court means to try to attract for mating. Male quetzals court females by flying in a special spiral pattern. First, the male flies straight up into the air. After this, he turns quickly and flies straight back down. This shows the female that the male is ready to mate.

Some scientists think that quetzals mate for life. Once a male quetzal has found a female mate, the two birds build a tree-hole nest together. The female lays two light-blue eggs inside the nest. The male and female quetzals take turns sitting on the eggs to keep them warm until they hatch.

Young Quetzals

After about 18 days, the eggs hatch. Newly hatched quetzals are called chicks. The little chicks have pink skin and no feathers. When they are born, they are very hungry. The mother or father quetzal brings food to the nest to feed the chicks. Without feathers, the chicks cannot keep themselves warm. One parent stays in the nest to keep the chicks warm, while the other parent hunts for food.

Chicks are born with their eyes shut. After about eight days, their eyes slowly open. At this time, they also have enough feathers to keep themselves warm.

For about the next four weeks, the chicks stay in the nest. The parents take turns bringing their chicks small lizards, snails, and insects to eat. The parents also guard the nest from other animals.

Chicks are in danger when they are young. Larger birds, such as toucans, eat quetzal chicks. Other animals, such as snakes, weasels, and coatis, will try to steal and eat quetzal eggs or chicks.

Chicks leave the nest when they are about one month old. By that time, they have small tail feathers and can fly short distances. For about

This female quetzal is feeding fruit to her young chick.

the next month, they live in the rain forest with their parents. The parents help the chicks find enough food to eat. When the chicks are about two months old, they leave to find their own territories.

Then the male and female quetzals go back to living on their own. The next spring, they will find each other to raise more chicks.

Scientists think that quetzals live for 15 to 20 years.

A Quetzal's Day

Quetzals are **diurnal**. This means they sleep at night and are active during the day.

Quetzals awaken in the morning inside their nest. They spend most of their day flying around their territory to look for food. At night, they return to their nest to sleep.

Quetzals spend a small part of each day preening. Preening is cleaning their feathers. Quetzals use their beak to comb out their feathers. By doing this, they keep their feathers straight and clean. They would have problems flying if they had crooked or dirty feathers.

Quetzals travel mostly by flying. This is because they do not walk very well. They have very short legs and cannot move quickly with them.

Since quetzals cannot walk very well, they do not spend much time on the ground. They live in the treetops of the rain forest. This area of thick leaves and branches is called the forest **canopy**.

The quetzal's green color helps keep it camouflaged among the leaves of the canopy. **Camouflage** is special coloring or patterns that help an animal blend in with its surroundings. Still, quetzals are in danger from some predators. A predator is an animal that hunts other animals for food. Even with the camouflage, not all quetzals live to be adults. Predators catch many of them in the first year or two of their lives. People also hunt them for their feathers.

In ancient times, it was against the law to kill quetzals. People caught them and took some of their feathers. Then, they let the birds go again.

The Future of Quetzals

Quetzals were important birds to ancient people. The **Mayas** were a group of people that lived in Central America thousands of years ago. Only kings and other Mayan leaders could wear clothes with quetzal feathers on them.

The Mayas and other ancient people in Central America often used feathers as money. They traded feathers for gold and other objects. Of all the kinds of feathers, quetzal feathers were the most valuable. To be valuable means to be worth a lot of money.

Today, quetzals are still very important in Central America. In the country of Guatemala, the quetzal is the national bird. Money in Guatemala is called a quetzal. There are pictures of quetzals on both the money and the flag of Guatemala.

You can see the quetzal bird in the left corner of this Guatemalan money.

What Will Happen to Quetzals?

Quetzals are rare, **endangered** birds. Endangered means a species of animal might die out. Quetzals are endangered because their natural rain forest habitat is being destroyed. People are cutting down trees in the rain forest to build homes, farms, and roads, and to sell

Many people in South America say that a quetzal cannot live if it has been captured. They say it will die of a broken heart. Because of this, the quetzal has become a symbol of freedom in South America.

wood. Without rain forest trees, quetzals will have no homes and no way to find food.

Quetzals are also in danger from hunters. Some people try to catch and kill quetzals. They sell quetzal feathers and skin.

Some people are trying to save the quetzal. They are working to make it against the law to cut down rain forest trees. There are special parks where quetzals can live. Hunting is against the law in these places. Today, all six of the countries where quetzals live have special parks.

More work is needed to save the rain forest. Some people try to teach others how to use the land without destroying it. Then, the rain forest can remain a home to many animals, including the resplendent quetzal.

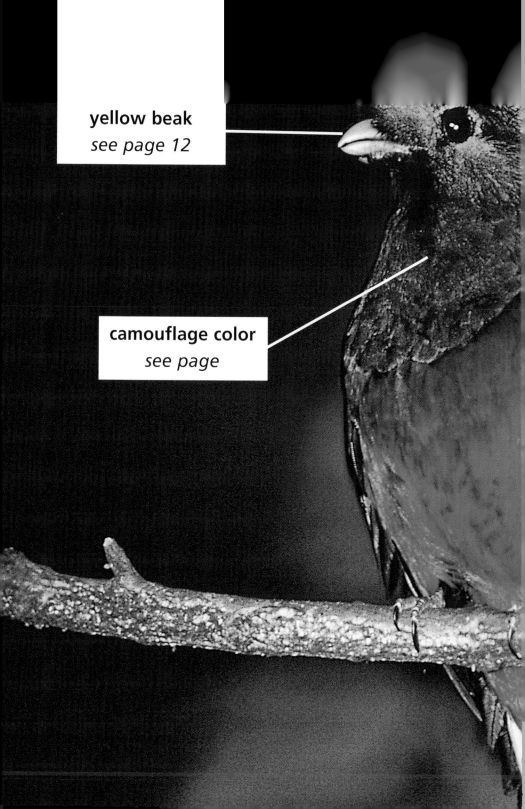

yellow beak
see page 12

camouflage color
see page

crest
see page 13

wings
see page 13

long tail feathers
see page 13

Glossary

camouflage (KAM-o-flaj)—colors, shapes, and patterns that help an animal blend in with its background

canopy (CAN-oh-pee)—the area of the rain forest with thick leaves and the most branches

coverts (KOH-verts)—the four long green tail feathers found on a male quetzal

diurnal (dye-UR-nal)—animals that sleep at night and are active during the day

endangered (en-DAYN-jurd)—when a species of animal may die out

habitat (HAB-i-tat)—the place where an animal or plant usually lives

Mayas (MY-ahs)—a group of people that lived in Central America thousands of years ago

migrating (MY-gray-ting)—to move to a new habitat when the season changes

omnivores (AHM-nee-vohrz)—animals that eat both plants and animals

predators (PRED-uh-turs)—animals that hunt other animals for food

Internet Sites

Cloud Forest Alive: QuetzalCam!
www.cloudforestalive.org/tour/qcam/

Quetzal
www.animalsoftherainforest.org/quetzal.htm

Useful Address

Rain Forest Action Network
221 Pine Street, Suite 500
San Francisco, CA 94104

Books to Read

Palacios, Argentina. *The Hummingbird King.*
New York: Troll Associates, 1993.

Patent, Dorothy Hinshaw. *Quetzal: Sacred Bird
of the Cloud Forest.* New York: Morrow Junior
Books, 1996.

Index